Plat

Lindsey Webb

ADVANCE PRAISE

"At once phenomenological and grounded, vast and detailed, Lindsey Webb's *Plat* renews my faith in language. Its contours remind me of Rosmarie Waldrop's *Curves to the Apple*, but *Plat* finds a grammar all its own. An exquisite debut collection."

—CLAIRE DONATO

"Every time I open Lindsey Webb's *Plat* it reveals itself to be something uncannily different, so much so that I am beginning to understand it as being exactly that: an environment composed of the many facets of its personality constantly shifting, i.e. a book-length spinning jenny, the translation of the self-consciousness of moving through a succession of interiors in the absence of the one who is waiting, elegy and augury, just for starters. And because it is poetry, I understand it also as the realization that grief is dimensional (architectural, horticultural), the design and cultivation of the afterlife."

—BRANDON SHIMODA

"The three poems of *Plat*—'Garden,' 'Mancala,' and 'House'—constitute a tripartite movement through mourning as though to move beyond it, but equally in terror and in thrall one remains snagged on the thorny subjunctives of these premises. Snagged on the as-though. 'I crawl,' Webb writes, 'in the interest of the dead.' This calamitous book treats grief even as it assays the estate of the Real. The poet's instruments: a burnished language of the uncanny, 'a veiled approach toward a sentence,' and a 'collaps[ing] inward toward the future, away from all frontiers.' I am deeply affected by Lindsey Webb's necropastoral."

—ADITI MACHADO

"Lindsey Webb's *Plat* explores brutal loss through the lens of a failed utopia, with each poem crafted like a careful prayer. 'I've not opened your letters. I've not kept your laugh fresh,' the speaker admits, leading us out of an ethereal garden and into a house where death is reluctantly accepted. In *Plat*, heaven is an ever-changing, manmade structure where pain and suffering persist, with hope nothing more than a whisper. Webb creates lines with careful brush strokes, each more devastating than the last."

—LAUREN MILICI

"In *Plat*, Lindsey Webb surveys the dream space of grief. By delimiting the reader's view to the geographical, philosophical—even ecological—dimensions of her own personal loss, Webb pushes sentiment out of the grid. Much like Lucretia Martel's film, *The Headless Woman*, *Plat* interrogates capitalism, collective cultural life and religion through the unrealized dreams of Prophets, the unspoken words of the dead, and the violent bang and clatter of an accident that's always held unseen. *Plat* is the perfect song for our dystopian world and Lindsey Webb, the singer of our utopian dreams."

—GEOFF RICKLY

"In Webb's brilliant book *Plat* a story unfolds in plants and in futures that do not exist. The poems ask, is there room for death in the utopia? Is there room for any of us in the plat, in the house, or in the garden? Reading this stunning collection reinforces that loss is both collective and connecting. Together we are in the house and together we are hurting. Windows, walls, all feeling."

—LA WARMAN

Published in the United States by:
Archway Editions, a division of powerHouse Cultural Entertainment, Inc.
32 Adams Street
Brooklyn, NY 11201
e-mail: info@powerHouseBooks.com
website: www.archwayeditions.us

Daniel Power, CEO
Chris Molnar, Founder and Editorial Director
Nicodemus Nicoludis, Founder and Managing Editor
Naomi Falk, Senior Editor
Caitlin Forst, Contributing Editor
Mia Risher, Publicist

Edited by Naomi Falk

Library of Congress Control Number: 2023950659

ISBN 978-1648230622

Printed by Toppan

First edition, 2024

10 9 8 7 6 5 4 3 2 1

Cover art: Johann Michael Rottmayr. *Allegory of Architecture* (detail). 1705-08. Fresco.
Liechtenstein Museum, Vienna

Printed and bound in China

ARCHWAY
EDITIONS

Plat

Lindsey Webb

Archway Editions, Brooklyn, NY

for Swenson

CONTENTS

*

Joseph Smith's "Plat of Zion" is a drawing of a plan for a celestial city on Earth, which he said was shown to him in a vision.

The plat's center holds twenty-four "houses of the Lord": buildings of worship, centers for community gathering, and places of education.

The city center is ringed by a grid of residential plots. This grid is ringed by fields and farmlands.

The plat would simplify equitable distribution of resources and cultivate community cohesion. No spaces on the plat were reserved for commerce.

GARDEN

Locke sank into a swoon;
The Garden died;
God took the spinning-jenny
out of his side.

—W. B. Yeats

Before you died, I confused the personal with the ecological, die with dye. Now I hold my mouth to the mouth of a tree and blow. Was I died here too, or did I born? I call the rabbits whatever comes into my head, though a pearly vapor rolls beneath the real. Deep fur behind a name.

Sitting in a garden, unsheltered from the moon's ongoing description of the sun. A coyote walks up to a flowering pear and sticks her head in. Hibiscus spends at least part of the night describing the moon.

If heaven will arrive one day on earth, as Joseph Smith said, will it appear as a grid? If women don't speak to God directly, what will they say when heaven falls to earth like a curtain? What will be in their mouths? You float past me above the leaf duff, "clean" like a ghost, "clean" like a difficult vessel.

The garden is not a nightmare: it hallucinates itself each season. Where's my dream and where's my cultivation? Death or capital? I remember weedkiller was born of a man's desire, so I can't address my femininity in a garden. Too expensive. A $20 barrette at the corner of my face; a freak double-headed rose. Here every flower might be a rose.

The garden builds up the natural exactly as fast as it disintegrates. I read in my exercise book that with enough practice one can access the overtone sequence, "in which each frequency is an integer multiple of a fundamental." Guitar music, violin music; there must be a quicker door. But this entire place aspires to allegory. The catalpa, too, with help from the fugitive wind, has decided to escape its plot.

Everywhere I plant theories about your death they come up several months later sticky and rotting from the inside with motive.

An apple tree painted on the wall looks like a plan. I walk over, as if to confront illustration. I pretend to cup the fruit in my hand and pull it back, pluck it from the tree, lift it into the third dimension. I drop it by relaxing my fingers. But the red fruit remains an argument kept closely to the wall, still red. My reply is overdrawn, and I reach out, attempt to pay again.

Winter comes to the garden, then fall, then summer. Hours construct themselves exactly as fast as they disintegrate. I came here to read and speculate but forgot how I got in. Ants imply distance to cover; death implies time has gone on without you; I should start over. Maybe I'll go into real estate. You place your finger lightly on a string, and the garden hits a different octave. I put on a face like a window and walk around the plat. I'm waiting for the northern cardinal to catch his reflection in my countenance, to wear himself out fighting it.

There's a middle and an end but no beginning. What they call the "pre-mortal existence." Though I swear I saw you firmly in the beginning of the garden, bending to tell a secret to a tree.

What does your memory have to do with abstract space? When you were alive things were bad, regular. After surgery you came to me in the garden. I was digging, what, marigolds?, and you said "so this is happiness."

Meanwhile the garden, firmly in a dead future. Meanwhile the end, stitched to a marigold, firmly post-mortal. You could tell when I was being sarcastic. You held your face, unrelenting, between.

In working the garden I've rinsed away the soft contours of my own faith, so that color is the only ornament. Texture's catchy loss. Here there are no doors but little subdivisions, a sensation of the ancient on a plate. They tell me disgust comes only from the ground up, as if it weren't ingested on the wing and left to shunt, tunneling into the gut. As if I didn't come here with doubts.

Within days I sit in a circle talking, against a daylily. At first I chat about your young death, echoing the sentiment of a "new sister-hood," as if the garden had no structure. Just a cloud of light. Then violet, fugitive scent, brings me to myself. They ask, "what can we do to prevent deaths like hers?" I stay quiet and scrape the plat. I find shafts, beams, I discover, what, a new luminescence? No: centipedes, reforming loss, lattice of rot and raw matter, nailed into planks. A pink wilderness of sod and infrastructure.

The garden tells its lie of isolation: "nature has died and the garden is its memory." A cool blanket of irrigation pools in the corners of each leaf. Ghosts and rabbits, horned lizards, carpenter ants organize their respective diplomatic anarchism. I take a different path, almost running—disturbed by all the roses facing forward, as if I'd set them out myself.

When we were younger, I complained I had no sisters. You, taller and prettier, turned your darker hair around a finger. In a silly voice, you said: remember, I'm your sister.

Older, I forgot. I, forgetter.

An ant breathes, pauses. The ant thinks, and I think. I think the garden preserves the pages of books, rather than vice versa. The oil of flowers writes in empty loops, slow beneath the English. Before you died, I could imagine a book's fourth dimension—the dimension of stain, skipper of pages. Now the ant enters a tunnel it built itself, and the garden rotates around it like a thread around a spool.

Another path unwinds, then splits.

I dig, mulch, prune, and fertilize, I don't dig, mulch, prune, and fertilize. I grow you; I die you. In my dream I visit a time before your death, when nature generated itself from a spool of tiny spirals. Little white berries. I'm told the garden is wherever the righteous are, or vice versa; so at the felled catalpa I follow a vein of pollen, adopt a mastic attitude. I eat something that looks delicious but has no taste. Meanwhile, over my shoulder, a young woman sucks at the sap of a tree, bending as if permanently cast that way, shrouded in the blue light of archetype.

Even in shadow the garden's washed and washed with color until it glows with a special kind of light, as if radiating from the category itself.

I find near the wall a pink-headed duck, taxidermied and on display away from direct light. Extinct pink. It's difficult to describe loss from the other side of a glass. Are there areas where pink rots? Little inlets where the natural pigment, exposed to light, has fled like a fugitive? I'm told these suggest some hybrid world.

Last year's seed sprouts from a silo padlock. The accident of owner-ship issues a market. The problem of objects in the garden becomes not what they are, beneath their watery surfaces, but who husbands them. They tell me a tree has nothing to have; meanwhile I labor under the shade of reciprocity. Trim, mow, own. I imagine the world exactly as it is, then heaven as a grid overlaying it. Sin of omission instead.

They tell me the garden synonym, beauty. I say the right word is worms. They tell me to find a happy medium; I say the garden has no medium because it is not common. I mean not held in common. What I don't say is that it keeps its fugitive unknowns beneath the topsoil. Its medium is elsewhere, cherished as a lost species.

At the split-leaf philodendron I turn left. Even the wilderness has us in it, as its off-stage opposite.

Meanwhile the kitchen takes its orders from the garden: tropics goes to temperate goes to tropics. In this way, agriculture asserts its regional dominance over my stomach. Nobody is in here except us, remember? And cultivation is coincident with desire. Spiced aromatic green herb sauce. Roseate squash, adrift in a pool of clear butter; fragrant and rapidly cooling.

The garden is not an allegory; it aspires to curl out. You told me you wanted to be buried young and beneath some tree. When you died the world turned sketchy, as I mistakenly thought the garden brooked no death. I forgot the coyote head: trapped face-up in the grate, washed there by the spring floods, suspended by the jaw. And me, too—I say I will uncapture, but I eat and eat.

In meandering I become a bit of leaf matter, a hollow snail shell. Once I saw a young woman walk up to a scrub oak and put her mouth on it. Was it a kissing game, a couple transferring gum between their mouths? Did she murmur into the ear of the planet? She looked like you—maybe you were practicing the flute, an instrument you never learned. Silent flute above the pretty sound of water.

The garden is not beautiful; it is totally unsuitable for the raising of temples. Its location is desolate and difficult to access. The dead release their new data every year: not easy. Not nothing. How I wish, sometimes, there were bunches of nothing. Snow falling on berries in a line of soft *no's*. I remember your old sentences strangled, tore, died quickly...then lashed out in opposite directions.

Let's return to the eccentric square. Let's fall back and regroup over lunch. You collect purple globes from the plum tree, and they melt tasteless on my palate. To what border did you flee, anthocyanin? "A fucked-up building?" Madder root, rot of the subject…I forget what I was saying. Here, economies of grids predominate; here there's neglect and weird collapse. I walk on all fours in a cloud of surplus. I crawl in the interest of the dead.

*

Should population reach capacity, another plat could be built imme-diately adjacent to the first, and another after that, "and so fill up the world" (Smith). This idea operated under the assumption that fertile, even terrain was endless—and empty, which it was certainly not. Mor-mons were violently reminded of this by non-Mormon settlers in Missou-ri, who saw poison in the plat.

Despite Smith never realizing the plat, nor the utopian ideals which un-dergirded it, many later cities built by Mormon settlers internalized its shape. Heaven changes over time: the plat's mode of conquest as self-rep-lication is preserved into the future. The plat's other, less "productive" modes, its anti-capitalism, are left behind. Only a skeleton lingers: the poison marching grid, and buried deep within it, something like an an-tidote.

MANCALA

*Walk into this building and you
walk into a purposeful guess.*

—Gins and Arakawa

Everywhere I look I see interests.

Walking barefoot over the plat I spend the rest of the morning pulling splinters from
 my feet.

 I speak to you, say I made it with fresh milk,

then hand you something I can't see.

 You turn it in your hands

in the light like a pearl.

 Some portraits have interests in resource extraction. To avoid this, I hide

your pictures

behind the hedge.

 I am not successful.

 You move to the side of the swimming pool and fold your wet

arms on the tiles, rest

 your head on your wrists.

They tell me to build a narrative of your death.
I find a seashell in a hollow tree, pretending nothing is as it shouldn't be: things just are.
    You just died.
    I try for a moment to write just the facts.
    A coyote finds a patch of familiar piss
and rolls in it.
    One sentence goes: "It's possible heaven killed her." Though I've learned "a sentence
    is an interval during which if there is a difficulty they will do
away with it."
    Sheets drop one after another to the edge of the yard, beyond.
    You tell me at the horizon is where they tie
the sky down.
    The wall billows like laundry on a wire, plucked,
gathered up, then dropped.

I follow a machine of inputs and outputs, like a hallway to an earlier thought.
Purple lights move across the hedge and wrap around my throat.

    When I crack the door in the garden wall, an arithmetic: carrying
the one, carrying the two.

    The ice cubes in my glass splinter when you show
me a hallway.

    Entering, they ask me to tell the story of your death. I make
an attempt:

        genetic predisposition
        untreatable condition
        intentional overdose

    Fenced, not trapped. Herded.

    A coyote follows me, a coyote made of intersecting planes. I have met her before,
in the so-called "pre-existence."

    I rotate my camera to the right and see my reflection.

    To the left: girl teenager
in a lousy heaven.

    I try to enter it but, being a coyote, it remains
closed to me.

A hallway made of stacked lines leads to my room.
At the sound of loud music I condense vertically like a sheaf of wheat.

    I write, *A young woman pisses in the yard, and the stones
froth; get holy.*

    All this time you sit on my sofa and laugh at me, as I stumble over my own
speech.

    Yards, colors, root matter, heaven's purchase on a plate.

    I stretch across your memory and, with enough effort,
flatten and expand.

    Like a purple reflection on a glass sea, a thin surface of ink,
a kind of double mountain.

    They tell me to build a narrative of your death that exonerates them, but I don't
know where to find innocence.

    When I ask, they respond: *you've
forfeited.*

A lake of blue where my arm used to be.

The garden, at my back, still encourages me to speculate:

hair and beauty products

heaven's bad mood

the manful ordering of things

Standing far enough back I get your reasons mixed up with mine, a vague transfer of ownership.

Wash of unbound colors.

They tell me markets predict the future, and therein retain a kind of innocence.

I run my hand over the stone wall, blank and undirectional.
When you died my life became a grid with many points but no way.

Thankfully, the garden keeps giving me envelopes: red for my hospital bills, yellow for my investments.

On the other side of the wall a woman plays her saxophone the way one might shuffle cards.

Her C# has a torn corner.

I open a door to splinter the apparently seamless barrier
between cause and effect.

· Though I make a crack big enough to slip through, I am, on the whole, closing.

The plat goes on hoarding its future like a sucked-in breath.

I put clay to my eyes and swallow.

Little root nodes follow me along the rock wall like points of light.

My heart, once angry and brittle, softens like a young
sculpture.

In my next sculpture, young wine.

Caught out late in a downpour, my thin shirt completely soaked, the world
melts into a thin membrane.

They say assigning motive is different than telling a story, as heaven
is different from the earth.

I once saw you tear a page perfectly so that the image pulled away
from the paper beneath.

Meanwhile a sentence becomes a lit hallway leading to another lit hallway.

A coyote travels in a straight line toward its point.

But I consider escaping through the second life of description, that illusory, placid
valley which springs up when looking at a single mountain cross-eyed.

Clay-rinsed.

I feel for a little shape with the toe of my boot, open a soft barrier,
then step, as a visit—

Crowds of people milling on the portico.

You stand off to the side, splitting wood into perfect wedges, as if we were alone
    in the country.

    Someone brings me rosemary from the garden and I rub some
beneath my jawline

    and across my wrists.

    A sprig, a collection of flexible polyhedrons—something buckles
in the wind.

    The coyote collapses inward like a house
of cards when I call out.

    Why?

    If the sky is the mood, you suspend across my unanswered question
like a net of thunderheads:

    Purple; immediate. Grid for an answer.

HOUSE

*I'm into the way
the technology of an I
is filled with the dead.*

—Peter Gizzi

*See now, I dwell in an house of cedar, but the
ark of God dwelleth within curtains.*

—2 Samuel 7:2

When I first considered my career in time, the house installed its kin. Busy setting up for the party, I thought they weren't organs. I thought I had a purse. In your photograph, a white door dries in the morning sun, though in my memory it was red. It bursts into hives when I talk about it, and telescopes my relation to the true.

A shame the house lies within the framework of the real. Though knowing remains the irritant of knowledge. And I still hesitate at the threshold of sisterhood. Who are all these people come to meet me? When violence arrives at the house, it will appear as a woman waiting her knowing out. As wallpaper at the banister's foot. As a pause—a nail—a lily smell on paper. Space heals nothing yet, or only in red strips.

Whisper of machine; loud laughter. I move from room to spiritroom with some difficulty. In this way, the house is all bibles. Literature cups the cheek of an old woman, rendered in glass, looking down on the gray-haired room. No need to tell you a machine has entrances and exits, and the spirit of a machine has volume. A spinning-jenny greets me at the center of the house.

The house is not a metaphor: it orients against death. I've adopted this position myself after some convincing. When you died I installed a mirror which fed me back in concentrated streams my own voice. Nothing withheld, just dirt floor, violin music: your negative translation. Photographs of each possible haircut in a sunshape around the door. A carpet where no one had stepped.

Here reminds me of the world. Of sewing my life to a curtain, and a hand behind it. This reminds me of raw material, antechamber; a shaking door for spiders, wood that has the spirit handshake. Does it lead me in, or above? Can I get back from it, get out on the porch, get a good look?

They say feet carry the mind, as trees can carry concepts. Windows here dump faces onto faces, lift the vellum from the words. They say I have entered the enter; that to enter the world of baptism is easy, the world of paneling difficult. Little blond tables. I'll describe what I see: heaven, a young woman with her back turned to the future, a little lesson.

Even though I'm on my period I'm permitted a white ritual jumpsuit. I'm allowed the wet touch of ghosts. Even though the house is surveilled I am mutual, and a cat falls out of the wall, landing on my shoulders. Even the curtains of power are satin beneath. Even rooms are natural, odd rooms plastic. I should have known that, going in. A ghost touches the cat and she bursts into paint, slicked on the water like a shade.

It has an appetite for every goodly thing. I swim through coats and shoes, stumble onto card games on the stairs. Someone brings me a gift—lightmindedness, a candle in the late, dark house.

How does the house desire me? I sit in a soft chair among the group, and a coyote bites her own ankle. I've been asked to ponder as a market ponders. When a child comes to the window to kiss it, I posit: *It desires my time.* The coyote always dies, dies again; a satin duration. A scolding: *Things do not appear from nowhere,* though an aloe leaf suddenly colors my hand. This will impede my progress. My desire colors the next room.

Stairs carry air up and down, because the house expects my step. I read the carpet sentences with my gait. The banisters are pure apple, brought over from the next town; the paintings are pure reproduction, poorly done. The latticed porch took seven generations. The windows—well, nothing can be done about the windows. The windows leak tears. The windows are an open topology.

I've got a feeling about this life, and that is that I carry the living, while the dead carry me. If they drain out I'll collapse inward toward the future, away from all frontiers.

Once you said "if you slow your breathing, you slow your heart." Your fish kept behind glass kept mouthing it. I've not opened your letters. I've not kept your laugh fresh. Targeted marketing for the grieving has defiled the little I've kept; photography has burnished the rest. Think of a ball bearing; now, move a piano with it. Slide this heavy thing across a sheet of tiny spheres. This is how you, the dead, move.

Now love melts fruit into broth and forms an accidental lattice. That is the house's perfect fashion: its signal attenuates over time. A piano note degrades the second it's struck. A hallway measures time while a memory of an ancient place, Wyoming or Denmark, bleeds it.

A coyote, weeping in the field of the hallway. *I have— I have— I have— lost my faith.* She will not let me touch her, so I shout across the foyer, the cereal grasses: *maybe someone took it from you.*

Though I try to move beyond a simple "there is," I can't disregard the map. For example, in the top right corner "there is" a young person standing on the couch, putting on their pants, quickly checking the cat. In the bottom left corner, an old man in denim touches the grass of the yard. Sleep is also not without narrative. Purl of radio, yellow domestic shorthair. Each night, the floors of the house rearrange. Each morning beetles pour from the edge of the "there is."

The sky is exactly the color it is; a curtain reminds me of nothing. I pull in my arms and legs and float unconnected through the building, taking up the headspace—though the building accommodates this too. The house accommodates an everyone. Still, I get in the way. I displace the light; I am structurally unsound. When I try to speak analogy comes back like a coyote at the door, pissing on the hallway rug.

The house has no language of ownership, though it does have a language of material. Empty room, full room. The machine is a kind of argument: it digests me as I move. The latticework and colonnades enzyme my mood, a manticore falls, and then my plans degrade. My hand, when pressed against the corner of a table for a few moments, receives the spirit of the table as a temporary gift.

(Though "my" is a funny way of putting it. Implying an impression can be made on glass like water. Imagine a world where glass is artificial, and water is not. Imagine putting a priesthood key on the coffee table, just right there, and then walking out in complete forgetfulness. I swear it was. Was a complete way of putting it. Down, face down, right on the table. Right there.)

Do you know what I'm talking about when I say a woman takes my hand and whispers *here is where you may begin.* Where Beethoven's *alla turca* becomes the irritant of Mozart's. Without encouragement after a death a room begins to question itself, its choices over the years, its errors and embarrassments. This is the way of all architecture; it holds a dead plan at the joists.

I follow an ancestor behind the imitation gas lamps. Our association: mutual, buried like a structure under the dirt. Another entrance, waterless, washes me.

Power gives the other world a distinct cherry aftertaste. I wake up with ancestormouth. What sociality is this? What are the properties of our property? Some of us rent a hotel, others Wyoming. But tell me, who gently rips the plat from the center of the night? What it will take or give to let me in?

Trailing scarves of smoke, they keep all their effects in their hands. Keys on rings, cards, coins.

I imagine bending over to pick them up off the linoleum, one by one.

A nest of violets, teeming.

Slippery as a blood clot.

Where I forget your aspects, the building picks up the thread. It holds the memory of your body like a spirit in the bottom of a glass, a puff of dust when I blow into it. I almost envy you, being dead; I invite you into the room as if to infect you with my life.

Concepts unlearn themselves. A man takes my card. We can't speak to each other except through a curtain, a gateless gate, more correctly translated as *gateless barrier,* here *antechamberless.* Or in special circumstances, after some study, a *wind tower, left-handed painting. Hair against neck.* We can only forgive each other through a *vestibule.*

Gaps in understanding become lavender gaps, morello cherries. The porous rhythm of human sentences. They tell me they reserved space for the elevators of the future, and wouldn't you know they proof perfectly. I love that collective space reserves a hole. I love the sleeve of a miracle. Though I might be dead I dream elevators constrict my body the higher they go. This is a veiled approach toward a sentence.

It must be true what they say: that in giving myself to a built environment I've attenuated the tone of my own body. How else to explain the phosphorus spark from the cap guns of my childhood? Proper nouns drain from the world, even as new ones are installed. Snowmelt is becoming expensive. My covenants rearrange on the satin undersides.

The house wants me to arrive, and I arrive. At the highest point of the machine the floors open up, in a kind of reproduction: splenetic, like ripe squash. Walls peel away from me in strings. *Palpate for weakness,* they said, touch and rub. My hands sink through a rotten spot, open a breath seam. Overheated bale. The room shoots me to its point of excess, through, out and through.

At the new curtain the house touched my cheek, the wind had no pine limit. Dusky satin: a column of air, daub and wattle palace of air. My substances did a reel, a beetle crawled backwards. You've placed a screen here? Though we are with us, and I am with you, I reach beyond. Man, I'm crawling to get in. I'm wild to see the room. I'm entering and entering under the arch.

*

I take utopia and hold it in my hand as a stick of gum. I swallow it without chewing. Picture a stomach, chewing gum. Does heaven digest me, or I it? Though I have felt obligated to provide one kind of context here, this poem is not explanation: it is another grid.

NOTES

"I die you" (p. 27) is taken from Katrina Dodson's translation of "Brasília" by Clarice Lispector. "A sentence is an interval during which if there is a difficulty they will do away with it" (p. 44) is taken from Gertrude Stein's *How to Write*. "A pause— a nail— a lily smell on paper" (p. 56) paraphrases a line from Lyn Hejinian's *My Life*.

ACKNOWLEDGEMENTS

I owe an unrepayable debt to everyone who has supported me and this book, whose pages are insufficient to contain all your names. Thank you to my parents, Thomas and Peggy, and my siblings, Jared, Cameron, and Val. To Dallin, for your love and steadiness. Thank you to the Archway Editions team, especially Naomi Falk, for making this book possible and handling it with such generosity. To my teachers at the University of Utah, UMass Amherst, and BYU, especially Craig Dworkin, Dara Wier, Kimberly Johnson, Lynn Xu, Maeera Schrieber, Michael Mejia, Paisley Rekdal, and Wendy Wischer. Thanks to friends and fellow students who read some of these poems inside and outside of workshops and who helped me shape this book. To the Strawberry Committee. To friends at The King's English Bookshop and Prairie Lights Books. To Claire Donato, Aditi Machado, Lauren Milici, Brandon Shimoda, Geoff Rickly, and LA Warman. To friends and supports Alicia, Billy, Carson, Jack, Kylan, Maddison, Parker. Love forever to Maddie and Melissa, and to the Swenson family.

Sincere thanks to the editors and readers of the publications in which some of these pieces first appeared: *Biscuit Hill*, *Carolina Quarterly*, *Chicago Review*, *Denver Quarterly*, *Dusie*, *Interim*, *Inter|rupture*, *jubilat*, *New Delta Review*, *TENDE RLOIN*, *Typo Magazine*, and *Vestiges*. Thank you to Naomi Washer and Patrick Thornton at Ghost Proposal, who published a version of "House" as a chapbook in 2020, and to Nora Claire Miller, Kelly Clare, and Alyssa Moore for continuing to support it.

Portions of this manuscript were completed thanks to fellowships and residencies at the Vermont Studio Center and the Taft-Nicholson Center for Environmental Humanities at the University of Utah. Thank you to the administrators and donors who made my stays there possible.

To the mountains, to poetry, and to God who lives within them.

MORE FROM ARCHWAY EDITIONS

Archway Editions is a literary imprint of indie art book publishing company **powerHouse Books**, and is distributed to the trade by Simon & Schuster; our books can be found in fine indie bookshops around the world, or Amazon if you must.

To learn more about **Archway Editions**, please visit here:

...and stop by our sister imprints **powerHouse Books**:

...and **POW! Kids Books**:

For trade queries, visit Simon & Schuster:

Send us love letters, mash notes, or mindless musings to:
  - comments@archwayeditions.us
  - or by tethered phone line @ 212-604-9074 x 104
  - or by postal delivery to our publishing HQ in Dumbo, Brooklyn.
    Archway Editions
    c/o POWERHOUSE Arena
    32 Adams Street
    Brooklyn, NY 11201

Or alternatively to our research lab in Industry City, Sunset Park:
    Archway Editions
    c/o POWERHOUSE @ IC
    238 36th Street (bldg. 2)
    Brooklyn, NY 11232

Lindsey Webb is the author of the chapbooks *House* and *Perfumer's Organ*. Her writing has appeared in *Chicago Review*, *Denver Quarterly*, *jubilat*, and *Lana Turner*, among others. She lives in Salt Lake City, where she is a PhD candidate in Literature and Creative Writing at the University of Utah. She edits Thirdhand Books. *Plat* is her first book.